GW00499174

# Queens of Africa
# Learn to control anger

JudyBee
Dan Doodies

www.queensofafricadolls.com

.

First edition published in 2015
© Copyright 2015
Judy Bartkowiak, Dan Doodies and Fico Solutions

The right of Judy Bartkowiak, Dan Doodies and Fico Solutions
Fitzpatrick to be identified as the authors of this work has been
asserted by them in accordance with the Copyright, Designs and
Patents Act 1998.

All rights reserved. No reproduction, copy or transmission of
this publication may be made without express prior written
permission. No paragraph of this publication may be
reproduced, copied or transmitted except with express prior
written permission or in accordance with the provisions of the
Copyright Act 1956 (as amended). Any person who commits
any unauthorised act in relation to this publication may be liable
to criminal prosecution and civil claims for damage.

All characters appearing in this work are fictitious. Any
resemblance to real persons, living or dead, is purely
coincidental. Although every effort has been made to ensure the
accuracy of the information contained in this book, as of the
date of publication, nothing herein should be construed as giving
advice. The opinions expressed herein are those of the authors
and not of MX Publishing.

Paperback ISBN 9781780922409
ePub ISBN 9781780922416
PDF ISBN 9781780922423
Published in the UK by MX Publishing
335 Princess Park Manor, Royal Drive, London, N11 3GX
www.mxpublishing.co.uk
Cover design by www.staunch.com

Become a fan of Queens of Africa by visiting their website www.queensofafricadolls.com where you can buy Wuraola, Azeezah and Nneka dolls in both traditional Nigerian clothes and modern outfits with accessories.

You can also buy more Queens of Africa story books, comics, learning books and much more. Learn how the girls are given supernatural powers and become Queens, empowered to change their world and do good works just as you can in yours.

Queens of Africa celebrates being an African girl in the 21st century by drawing on the strengths and achievements of our ancestors and bringing them up to date to empower and inspire today's generation of African girls.

"Good morning children. This morning I'd like you to welcome Leo to Dreamland International. His family have just moved here so he doesn't know anyone. I'd like you to look after him during his first week Zafar as you're in the same class."

Zafar's friends looked at him with new respect. What an honour to be asked to look after a new pupil at school.

Zafar himself was a bit shy and wondered what he would be expected to do with Leo, who looked quite a bit bigger than him. Leo's eyes were darting about everywhere; he was overwhelmed by all the boys and girls. This school was much bigger than the one he'd come from.

As the children walked out of assembly, Zafar waited for Leo and went to shake his hand as he'd seen his father do at the hospital where he worked as a doctor. Leo ignored it and pushed past Zafar knocking him against the wall. He didn't want to be looked after by anyone. He wanted to be back at his old school with his friends. He hadn't wanted to move, it was his parents' idea to move closer to his Aunty who was ill.

In the classroom, Leo sat next to Zafar and took out his pens ready for the lesson. It was Mr Ajayi's science lesson and there was a poster on the wall showing a tree with its branches, trunk and roots.

ROOTS

NUTRIENTS

"I want you all to copy this drawing into your books please," instructed  Mr Ajayi. He noticed that Leo didn't have a Science book so he took one from his drawer and put it on his desk.

Leo muttered something. Zafar was shocked. They were all taught to be respectful of teachers at school. He should have thanked him, he thought. Zafar wondered whether he should say anything, after all, he was supposed to be helping him.

Suddenly there was a crash. Zafar looked round to find that Leo had thrown his book and school bag on the floor. Mr Ajayi quietly picked them up and put them back on his desk and carried on with the lesson.

At break time Leo continued to be naughty and every time someone tried to be friendly, he pushed them away or threw something at them. In the end they just left him alone.

Zafar was in despair, what could he do? He went to find his sister Azeezah, she would know. She was with her friends Nneka and Wuraola. "What do I do Azeezah? Leo just seems so angry all the time."

"He's just sad and lonely I expect" said Azeezah "he probably misses his friends."

"Well he's going the wrong way about making new ones" said Zafar, "no-one wants to go anywhere near him, yet alone make friends."

"Why don't you ask him about his old school?" suggested Nneka "where was it?" Nneka loves travelling and one day she wants to be a pilot and fly all over the world.

"I could ask him what computer games he likes," suggested Wuraola. Wuraola is very clever. In fact she won a scholarship to Dreamland International but her favourite pastime is playing computer games.

"Well if we want him to be friendlier we need to show him how, by being friendly to him rather than leaving him alone," said Azeezah. Azeezah is a peace maker and wants everyone to be friends.

They walked over to Leo. At first he turned his back on them and continued to kick the wall. They started to talk to him and he turned round and glared at them. He didn't answer their questions but kept kicking the wall with his foot. Their plan didn't seem to be working at all. But they carried on talking and smiling and showed they wanted to be friends. Nneka shared her crisps with him.

They asked him about his family. He told them that his older brother and sister had not moved with the rest of the family because they had jobs in the town where they had lived. He looked sad and lonely.

Azeezah had been right.

Then they asked him what he liked to do in his spare time, did he have any hobbies? Did he like sport?

They found out that he liked basketball so Zafar went to fetch one to play with.

Leo bounced the ball up and down the playground, in and out of the children playing and scored goal after goal. Then he started to pass the ball to Zafar and the girls and soon there was a great game happening as other children joined in.

Even Mr Ajayi came to watch them.

Leo started to smile and laugh as the other children played with him.

"You're really good," they said "You should be in the school team."

"I was in the team at my last school" said Leo. Suddenly he looked sad again. "But they told me I got too angry if we lost so I was dropped."

"Why do you get so angry" asked Wuraola kindly.

"I don't know, I just suddenly feel angry".

"What happens first?" asked Wuraola. She remembered reading about anger in a book that Judy Bartkowiak had left them when she came to the school to show them how to be confident. She read that it's important to find out what happens first, before someone gets angry.

"Well I sort of see red, colours seem stronger and then I get excited and nervous, my hands feel all hot and then I sort of lose control. It's almost as if everything's spinning around me. Then afterwards I feel really bad because I get into trouble and people don't like me. They don't want to be friends. But then that makes me angry all over again because I feel sad and alone and I get cross and upset all at the same time. I just don't seem to be able to stop myself."

"We learnt something that might help you with that, it's called anchoring. Do you want to give it a go? It will help you to stay calm."

"Yes please, will you teach it to me?" asked Leo.

So at lunch time the girls showed Leo how to anchor a calm state so he didn't get angry.

"First you close your eyes" Leo closed them. "Then you think about when you feel really calm and in control of your feelings." Leo thought about when he was with his Aunty because he had to be quiet and talk slowly when he was with her .

"Do you have a picture in your head, or is it a sound or an action?" asked Wuraola.

"It's a picture of my Aunty" said Leo. "As I picture her I feel relaxed and calm and we're having a nice chat.

"Then we'll call that picture your anchor," explained Wuraola.

"Now close your eyes again and picture your Aunty. Imagine you are with her and you feel completely relaxed and calm. Nothing is going to make you angry when you think of that picture of her."

Leo did the exercise again.

"Now whenever you want to feel calm. Say when you start to feel your hands getting hot or when things start to spin around you, imagine that picture in your head of your Aunty and you will be calm again" explained Wuraola.

"That's really helpful." Leo gave her a thumbs up sign. He really did look a lot more relaxed now.

"Friends", said Nneka "help each other so please could you help us with our basketball as we helped you with your anger. We can practise after school at my house.

"Of course," said Leo "perhaps if I use this anchoring I'll be able to join your Basketball team."

"Our basketball team," corrected Zafar.

"Perhaps with your help we'll all be in the team," laughed Wuraola.

Zafar took Leo's hand and together they ran off to their next class. Leo was happy that he had made new friends and learnt how to control his anger.

# INSTRUCTIONS
## ANCHORING EXERCISE

1. Decide what anchor will work for you. It could be a picture in your head like Leo's or a physical sign such as a 'thumbs up' sign or you could squeeze your earlobe.
2. Close your eyes and think about a time when you feel calm and relaxed.
3. Associate into the experience by making the memory very clear and strong.
4. When it is at its strongest, use your anchor.
5. As the memory fades, remove the anchor and break state – walk around a bit and give yourself a little shake.
6. Now do it again. Think of other times when you feel calm and relaxed and picture yourself in that state.
7. When the feeling of calmness is strong, use your anchor again.
8. As the feeling fades, 'break state' again.
9. Now think some more about feeling calm and repeat the exercise until every time you use your anchor you immediately feel in control and relaxed.

Use it whenever you want to be calm and not angry. Start to recognise the times when you are about to feel angry and use your anchor to feel differently. It's NLP in action!

Check out my blog

www.queensofafricabooks.com for new titles.

## Series 1

Queen Amina of Zaria

Queen Makeda

Queen Moremi

Queen Esther

Queen Idia

Madam Tinubu

## Series 2

Learn Confidence

Learn to make Friends

Learn to cope with Change

Learn how you Learn Best

Learn to be healthy

Learn to control anger

# Other books by JudyBee

*Danny goes to London*
*Danny Strikes Out In America*

Raising awareness and funds for the R.E.A.D.
program.

# Other Books By JudyBee

Lightning Source UK Ltd.
Milton Keynes UK
UKOW07f0156150617
303325UK00011B/59/P

9 781780 922409